In the City

Salvador Sarmiento

Illustrated with photographs

HAMPTON-BROWN BOOKS
MANY CULTURES, MANY LANGUAGES…MANY POSSIBILITIES!™

I can see the clouds
far, far away.

I can see the moon
far, far away.

I can see the buildings far, far away.

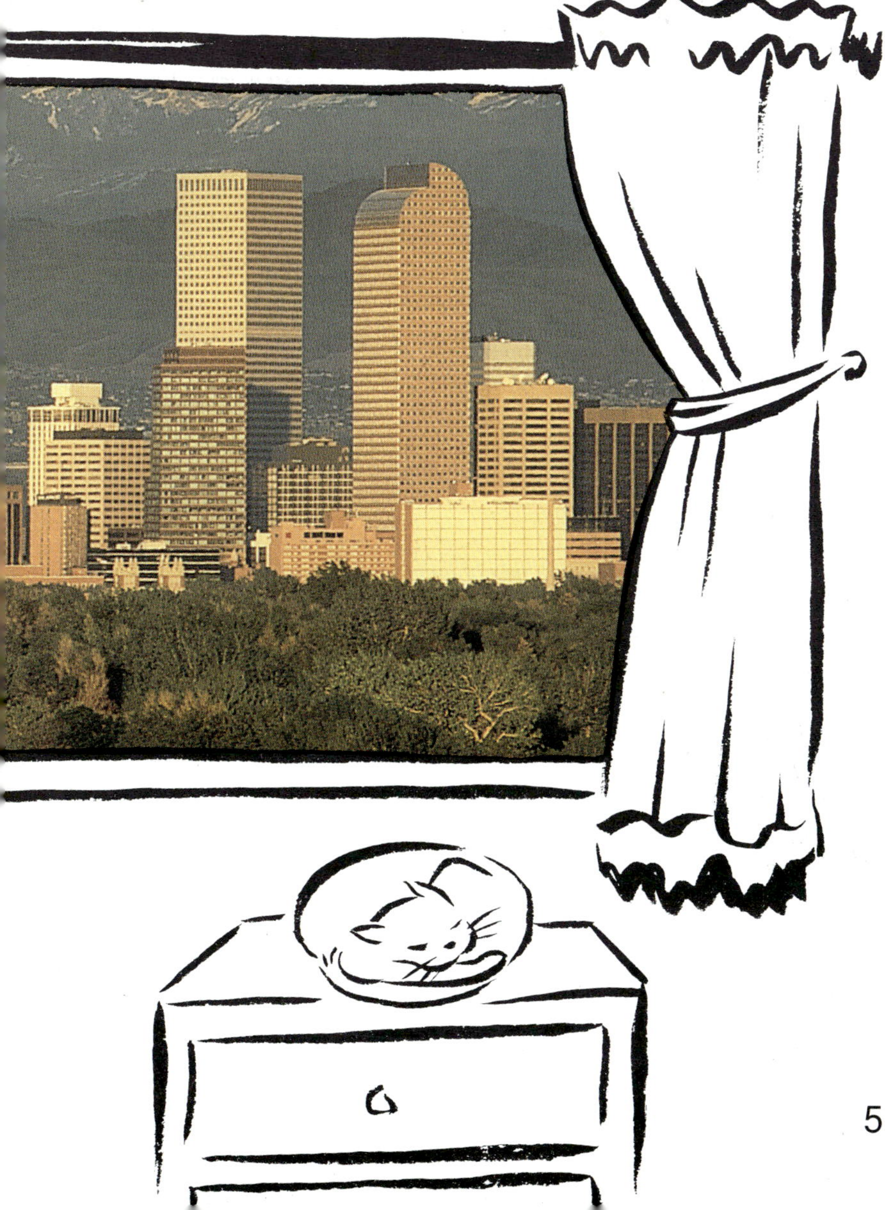

I can see the mountains far, far away.

I can see the lights
far, far away.

But I can see my mom
right here by me!

Necco® Sweethearts®

HAVE A HEART

Book of Friendship

By Kimberly Weinberger

Scholastic Inc.
New York Toronto London Auckland Sydney
Mexico City New Delhi Hong Kong Buenos Aires

If you purchased this book without a cover, you should be aware that this book is stolen property. It was reported as "unsold and destroyed" to the publisher, and neither the author nor the publisher has received any payment for this "stripped book."

No part of this publication may be reproduced in whole or in part, or stored in a retrieval system, or transmitted in any form or by any means, electronic, mechanical, photocopying, recording, or otherwise, without written permission of the publisher. For information regarding permission, write to Scholastic Inc., Attention: Permissions Department, 555 Broadway, New York, NY 10012.

ISBN 0-439-36539-2

Copyright © 2002 by New England Confectionery Company.
All rights reserved.   Published by Scholastic Inc.
NECCO is a registered trademark of the New England Confectionery Company.
Sweethearts is a registered trademark of the New England Confectionery Company.
SCHOLASTIC and associated logos are trademarks and/or registered trademarks of Scholastic Inc.

12 11 10 9 8 7 6 5 4 3 2 1   2 3 4 5 6 7/0

Printed in the U.S.A.
First Scholastic printing, January 2002

Have a Heart

She's the one you laugh with, talk with, shop with, dream with, and even fight with (though you always make up, of course). She's your best friend, and now here's a book for both of you to share.

Think you know everything there is to know about your best bud? Have you shared all there is to know about you? Well, here's your chance to record all the great stuff that makes your friendship so fantastic. Just grab that girlfriend, follow the yummy Sweethearts® conversation hearts, and let the fun begin!

Just the Facts

It's time to find out the 411 on you and your best bud. These are the basics that describe who you both are.

ME

Full name _____
Nickname _____
Address _____
Phone number _____
Birthday _____
Age _____
Eye color _____
Hair color _____

Paste or draw a picture of yourself in this box!

MY BEST FRIEND

Full name _____
nickname _____
Address _____
Phone number _____
Birthday _____
Age _____
Eye color _____
Hair color _____

Have your BF (best friend) paste or draw a picture of herself in this box!

LOVE YOU

First Impressions

How did you and your best friend meet? Was it "like at first sight," or did you need some time to realize you were meant for each other? Write down everything you

ME — How I first met _____

can remember about that day, then ask your friend to do the same. Compare your stories – are they exactly the same, or does one of you need a memory makeover?

IT'S LOVE

MY BEST FRIEND — How I first met _____

All in the Family

You may love her like a sister, but chances are your best friend isn't actually related to you. Fill in the names of your family members here.

ME

Mother's name _____

Father's name _____

Brothers and/or sisters

(Name) _____ (Age) _____

(Name) _____ (Age) _____

(Name) _____ (Age) _____

(Name) _____ (Age) _____

Pets _____

Grandparents' names _____
_____
_____

Aunts' names _____
_____
_____

Uncles' names _____
_____
_____

Cousins' names _____
_____
_____

Then, if you like, try covering your answers and see how much your friend knows about your family, and vice versa.

DEAR ONE

MY BEST FRIEND

Mother's name _____

Father's name _____

Brothers and/or sisters

(Name) _____ (Age) ____

(Name) _____ (Age) ____

(Name) _____ (Age) ____

(Name) _____ (Age) ____

Pets _____

Grandparents' names _____

Aunts' names _____

Uncles' names _____

Cousins' names _____

Who's That Girl?

How would you describe your best bud? Is she smart, sweet, and sensitive? Terrific, talkative, and totally together? List five words that fit your friend to a T.

ME

1. _____
2. _____
3. _____
4. _____
5. _____

then have her do the same for you. Did either of you choose any of the same words? Or are you two opposites that go great together?

AWESOME

MY BEST FRIEND

1. _____
2. _____
3. _____
4. _____
5. _____

Magazine Madness

If you and your best friend ever run out of words to describe how totally terrific you both are, try using someone else's. Go through your favorite magazines

Words that describe ME

Words that describe MY BEST FRIEND

together, and cut out any words that describe you, your BF, and your friendship. Paste them down below, and you'll have a mini-magazine that's all about you!

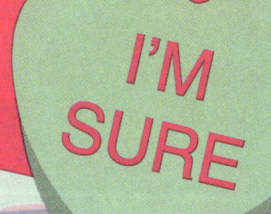

I'M SURE

Words that describe US

Time to Talk

You gotta love technology for keeping you and your best friend close. With phone calls, e-mails, and instant messages, you and your best bud can stay in touch 24/7!

ME

When I must get in touch with my best friend, I
- a) reach for the phone.
- b) send an e-mail.
- c) shoot off an instant message.
- d) other:

The best time of the day to talk on the phone is _____

My longest phone conversation ever lasted _____

I'm allowed to talk on the phone
- a) as long and as late as I want.
- b) as long as I want, but not after a certain time of night.
- c) My parents' rules about the phone are so strict, I may as well send a message in a bottle.
- d) other: _____

What's your favorite way to chat when you're not together? Does your BF agree? Fill in your thoughts below, and have your friend do the same.

CALL ME

MY BEST FRIEND

When I must get in touch with my best friend, I
    a) reach for the phone.
    b) send an e-mail.
    c) shoot off an instant message.
    d) other:

The best time of the day to talk on the phone is _____
_____
_____

My longest phone conversation ever lasted _____

I'm allowed to talk on the phone
    a) as long and as late as I want.
    b) as long as I want, but not after a certain time of night.
    c) My parents' rules about the phone are so strict, I may as well send a message in a bottle.
    d) other: _____
_____

What's in a Name?

Write the letters of your best friend's name down the side of the page. For each letter of her name, come up with a word describing how great she is. Does her

ME

Name	Description
___	_____
___	_____
___	_____
___	_____
___	_____
___	_____
___	_____
___	_____

name start with T for "terrific"? Or is it F for "fabulous"? Have your bud make the same type of list using the letters of your name.

FOR YOU

Name	Description
____	_____
____	_____
____	_____
____	_____
____	_____
____	_____
____	_____
____	_____
____	_____

MY BEST FRIEND

Sports Fan

Do you and your best friend love to race up and down the field, scoring big with the help of your teammates? Or does the idea of sports make you both want to run in

ME

When it comes to sports, I
a) love to play team sports.
b) prefer to play solo sports.
c) like to watch from the sidelines.
d) don't know a soccer ball from a hockey puck, and don't care to find out!

My favorite sports to play are _____

My favorite sports to watch on TV are _____

The sports figure I admire most is _____

If I could be great at any sport, it would have to be _____

The thing I like most about gym class is _____

If I could change one thing about gym class, it would be _____

the other direction? Not a problem! Team players or not, you know you'll always be there for each other!

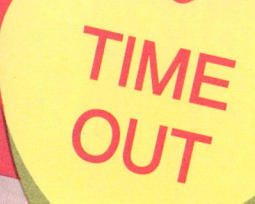

TIME OUT

MY BEST FRIEND

When it comes to sports, I
 a) love to play team sports.
 b) prefer to play solo sports.
 c) like to watch from the sidelines.
 d) don't know a soccer ball from a hockey puck, and don't care to find out!

My favorite sports to play are _____

My favorite sports to watch on TV are _____

The sports figure I admire most is _____

If I could be great at any sport, it would have to be _____

The thing I like most about gym class is _____

If I could change one thing about gym class, it would be _____

Take a Break

Where would you and your best friend go on your dream vacation? Whether you're swimming, surfing, or trekking across the North Pole, the important thing is that you and your BF will be totally together. Fill in the postcard below to tell the folks at home all about your amazing trip!

ONLY YOU

OUR DREAM VACATION TO _____

Music to My Ears

From pop and hip-hop to rock and rap, there's enough music out there to fit any girl's taste. How do you and your BF match up when it comes to your favorite tunes?

ME

My favorite song right now is _____

The song I'm completely sick of hearing is _____

The group or singer I love best is _____

My singing voice is
- a) worthy of a record deal — move over, Britney!
- b) mediocre — I can hold my own when I sing along with the radio.
- c) pretty awful — neighborhood cats start howling when I sing in the shower.

The instrument I play is _____

If I could play an instrument, it would be _____

Are your CD collections identical – or totally out of sync? Fill in your answers to the following questions and find out!

CUTIE PIE

MY BEST FRIEND

My favorite song right now is _____

The song I'm completely sick of hearing is _____

The group or singer I love best is _____

My singing voice is
 a) worthy of a record deal — move over, Britney!
 b) mediocre — I can hold my own when I sing along with the radio.
 c) pretty awful — neighborhood cats start howling when I sing in the shower.

The instrument I play is _____

If I could play an instrument, it would be _____

Page by Page

There's nothing like talking about a truly terrific book with your favorite friend. Whether you reach for romance, sci-fi, or anything in between, books are the

ME

The book I'm reading right now is
_____

The best book I ever read was
_____

My favorite author of all time is
_____

The type of book I like reading best is
a) mystery
b) romance
c) science fiction
d) fantasy
e) humor
f) horror
g) nonfiction
h) other

perfect place to lose yourself when you need a break. Just take a trip through the pages of a book (but don't forget to invite your BF along for the ride!).

COOL

MY BEST FRIEND

The book I'm reading right now is
_____

The best book I ever read was
_____

My favorite author of all time is
_____

The type of book I like reading best is
    a) mystery
    b) romance
    c) science fiction
    d) fantasy
    e) humor
    f) horror
    g) nonfiction
    h) other

Fashion Frenzy

What's your style? Do you and your BF match or clash? Page through some fashion magazines with your BF to find outfits you each like, then paste them down here.

MY STYLE

Or use this space to design an outfit that fits your unique style. Don't worry – whether you're totally trendy or completely casual, you still go great together!

IN STYLE

MY BEST FRIEND'S STYLE

School Stuff

So you're a whiz at math, and she's a history buff. Or maybe she's a mathemagician, while you go crazy for literature. Whichever way you slice it, you both have

ME

Name of school
_____

Grade _____

Teacher's name _____
_____

Best thing about my teacher
_____

Worst thing about my teacher
_____

Subject(s) I love
_____
_____

Subject(s) I could definitely do without _____

your favorite and not-so-favorite subjects when it comes to school. Fill in your thoughts below. And the best part? There's no grade given at the end!

GO GIRL

MY BEST FRIEND

Name of school
_____

Grade _____

Teacher's name _____
_____

Best thing about my teacher
_____

Worst thing about my teacher
_____

Subject(s) I love
_____
_____

Subject(s) I could definitely do without _____
_____

Homework Habits

It's an unavoidable fact of life: You're gonna have homework. How do you and your BF compare when it comes to getting those assignments done? Are you both the get-

ME

My favorite time to do homework is _____

My favorite place to do homework is _____

When I'm doing homework, I
 a) must have total silence.
 b) must have my favorite CD playing.
 c) must have the TV on.
 d) other:

The homework assignments I breeze through with no problem are _____

The homework assignments I could use a little help with are _____

My favorite person to call when I'm stumped by a homework problem is _____

because _____

it-over-with-quick type, or do you wait for the late-night hours before you crack open those books? Share your study secrets here.

YOU RULE

MY BEST FRIEND

My favorite time to do homework is _____

My favorite place to do homework is _____

When I'm doing homework, I
 a) must have total silence.
 b) must have my favorite CD playing.
 c) must have the TV on.
 d) other:

The homework assignments I breeze through with no problem are _____

The homework assignments I could use a little help with are _____

My favorite person to call when I'm stumped by a homework problem is _____

because _____

Have a Heart

Okay, you know your best friend is the greatest – but how often do you tell her that? And how often does your BF tell you

What I think about MY BEST FRIEND:

You're so **COOL** because _____

THANK YOU for _____

I HOPE you _____

URA STAR because _____

what a fantastic friend you are? Use these heart messages to fill each other in on how amazing you both are.

THANK YOU

What my best friend thinks about ME:

You're so **COOL** because _____

THANK YOU for _____

I HOPE you _____

URA STAR because _____

The Silver Screen

Big stars! Buttery popcorn! Sticky theater floors! Going to the movies with your best bud is a perfect way to spend a couple of hours (not to mention some big bucks,

ME

My favorite movie actor is
_____

My favorite movie actress is
_____

The best movie I ever saw was
_____

The worst movie I ever saw was
_____

I like to munch on _____ when I go to the movies.

The types of movies I like best are
a) comedy
b) horror
c) romance
d) drama
e) action/adventure
f) other

My least favorite type of movie is
_____

once you buy tickets, snacks, and drinks). Do you and your BF go wild for the same big-screen celebs?

STAR DUST

MY BEST FRIEND

My favorite movie actor is
_____

My favorite movie actress is
_____

The best movie I ever saw was
_____

The worst movie I ever saw was
_____

I like to munch on _____ when I go to the movies.

The types of movies I like best are
    a) comedy
    b) horror
    c) romance
    d) drama
    e) action/adventure
    f) other

My least favorite type of movie is
_____

TV Talk

Are you and your best pal in tune when it comes to TV? Do you call each other during commercials, and then again the moment your favorite show ends? Find out

ME

My favorite day of the week to watch TV is _____

My three favorite TV shows are
_____
_____
_____

The best actor on TV is _____

The best actress on TV is _____

If I could be a guest star on any TV show, it would be _____

because _____
_____

if you're both swept away by the same TV shows, or whether your tastes in the tube are as individual as you are!

URA STAR

MY BEST FRIEND

My favorite day of the week to watch TV is _____

My three favorite TV shows are
_____
_____
_____

The best actor on TV is
_____

The best actress on TV is
_____

If I could be a guest star on any TV show, it would be _____

because _____
_____

Shh! It's a Secret!

One of the greatest things about having a best friend is having someone to share all of your secrets with – without worrying that she'll blab them to the whole world.

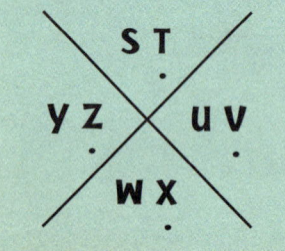

Use the outline of the box in which each letter falls as your new "alphabet." If you want to use the second letter in the box, just put a dot inside. For example:

I LIKE YOU becomes . . .

When it comes to your ultimate secrets, you need a language that's all your own. And now you have one! Just check out the grids below.

SWEET TALK

Use this page to practice writing messages to your BF. Ask her to do the same, and you'll both be secret code experts in no time!

For Your Eyes Only

Longtime crushes, embarrassing moments – there's nothing you can't tell your pal, and nothing she can't tell you. See if you can both answer the following questions

ME

My BF's secret crush is _____

My BF's most embarrassing moment ever was _____

The last time my BF cried was because _____

The worst day my BF ever had was _____

My BF's greatest secret wish is _____

about each other. Three right answers make you good friends, four make you best buds, and getting all five correct puts you in the Best Friends Hall of Fame!

ASK ME

MY BEST FRIEND

My BF's secret crush is _____

My BF's most embarrassing moment ever was _____

The last time my BF cried was because _____

The worst day my BF ever had was _____

My BF's greatest secret wish is _____

Party Pals

There's nothing like planning a party to bring two best friends together. Pick something to celebrate, and you're ready

WHEN: When will you have your party? Day or night, any time's the perfect time to celebrate with your BF!

WHERE: Where will you hold your party? Inside or outside? Your house or hers? Don't stress — wherever you go, you'll be together and that's what counts.

THEME: Is this a birthday party? A pajama party? Or maybe just an everyone-go-crazy-and-have-a-good-time party? It can be whatever the two of you want it to be — after all, you're in charge!

INVITATIONS: Make up an invitation list of all your best buds, then it's time to make your invitations. Make them as shiny, glittery, spangly, sparkly, and snazzy as you'd like. You want people to know that this will be a party to remember.

FOOD: Are you crazy for cookies? Does your BF love lemonade? Are you both suckers for sweets? Make a list of all your favorite snacks — and don't forget the NECCO® Sweethearts®!

to go! There are just a few minor details to figure out . . . .

BE TRUE

Once you've got all that figured out, there's only one thing left to do: Have a great time!

WHEN: _____
WHERE: _____
THEME: _____
FOOD: _____
_____

INVITATION LIST:
_____

_____
_____
_____
_____
_____

_____
_____
_____
_____
_____

Someday . . .

Your BF can understand all of your hopes and goals, no matter how far-out they may seem today. And you are always there to listen to her dreams, too. Share some of

ME

When I grow up I want to be a _____

_____

For me, the most important part of my future job will be
- a) the money.
- b) the fame.
- c) the happiness it brings me.
- d) being able to help other people.
- e) other: _____
_____

If I get married, the type of guy I'll choose will be _____

_____

If I have children, the number I'd like to have is _____

and I plan to name them _____

_____

I want to live in _____

because _____

Places I'd love to visit one day are:

_____

your dreams for the future here. Who knows? Years from now you may find that you've made all of your dreams come true.

DREAM GIRL

MY BEST FRIEND

When I grow up I want to be a _____

For me, the most important part of my future job will be
  a) the money.
  b) the fame.
  c) the happiness it brings me.
  d) being able to help other people.
  e) other: _____

If I get married, the type of guy I'll choose will be _____

If I have children, the number I'd like to have is _____
and I plan to name them _____

I want to live in _____
because _____
Places I'd love to visit one day are: _____

Time Travel

Will you and your friend be BFF (best friends forever)? What do you think your life will be like in the future? Imagine if you could travel through time to talk to your

Dear _____,

older selves – what would you say? Use the space below to write a letter to your best friend twenty years from now. Have your best bud write the same type of letter.

I HOPE

Dear _____ ,

Together Forever

Now that you and your best friend have finished this book, you should be closer than ever! Come back and visit the pages from time to time to see how you're both growing and changing. No matter what, one thing's for sure: You'll always be the best of friends!

Draw or paste a picture of you and your BF together in this box!

HUG ME

NECCO is a registered trademark of the New England Confectionery Company. Sweethearts is a registered trademark of the New England Confectionery Company. ISBN S-TK9-36539-2